MW01070282

Jane +
Henry here. The
S. @ farm.
ill celebrate
my 71 st
birthday
6-16-20

Jane Line Buckhorn (Fence)
3' from Fence - 3-4 ft. apart.
dont need to wrap in winter

Bailey Compact Cranberry
Viburnum (front of House
Vibr

Corner - Purple Smoke Tree
10' tall

Hydrangea   ↓

                    Also 2 front steps

Lights 3 X 36" order
        ↓
      strings

Electrician Estimate

K & B

Furniture Reupholstery 7/3/20

Kirby -
Came for measurement of
of chairs + ottomans

Gave note to keep welt
on both —

Also asked for estimate
on pillows.

Pick up + delivery ??

Cost —

July 2020

Twin City Trucking
$3000   Sewer & Water Line
                Replacement

Sidewalk $1400 (Curved front
~~$900~~   of house)
        Includes replacing
        city sidewalk

July 24, 2020   Brenda

Driveway - Matt   715-923-0533
           Corey

$5800
    includes removal of
    old.

End of Sept / Beg. Oct -
    2 pours -
    2-3 weeks -
                        cure
    7 days to dry
    after last pour

    1/2 down when end of
    end of day = Sept

mailbox

Lawn Care 2021 Dean

2020 House Projects -

ITEM	ESTIMATE	PAID DEPOSIT	AMOUNT DUE	PAID
Front Sidewalk	$1400.⁰⁰	$700 7-19-20 cash	($700)	$700 7-25-20
Upholstery	2306.28	$1306.28	($1000)	#6914 $1000 8-21-20
Sewer/Water	3000.⁰⁰	—	(3000)	√6899 $3000 #6899 8-2-20
Fence	5900.⁰⁰	$2500 √6831	(3400) → $3400 6-26-20	
Driveway	5800.⁰⁰	$2900 √ 7-30-20	($2900)	#6910 $2900 8-19-20
Misc Ray Plumbing	—		($18.44)	√6908 $418.44 8-14-20
Hookups Sewer/Water				
Permit - Sewer			($40)	$40
Permit - Sidewalk			($50)	$50

Made in the USA
Monee, IL
11 November 2019

16658075R00072